MW01120464

The Companion

Nikhil Pradip Joshi

Bloomington, IN Milton Keynes, UK

authorHOUSE®

AuthorHouse™
1663 Liberty Drive, Suite 200
Bloomington, IN 47403
www.authorhouse.com
Phone: 1-800-839-8640

AuthorHouse™ UK Ltd.
500 Avebury Boulevard
Central Milton Keynes, MK9 2BE
www.authorhouse.co.uk
Phone: 08001974150

First published by AuthorHouse 9/13/2006

ISBN: 1-4259-6120-7 (e)
ISBN: 1-4259-5806-0 (sc)

Printed in the United States of America
Bloomington, Indiana

This book is printed on acid-free paper.

For my mother, who put poetry in my heart,
my father, who told me to write it,
and to the One who loves me.

In the Beginning

I was nineteen when it happened.

I am an ordinary man. Nothing elevates me above those who have dwelt on this earth, those who live here now, and those who will come after me. I am ordinary.

I was a normal child, with beautiful good parents, excellent friends, and a full life. Like others, I made mistakes. I drank too much; I lusted; I occasionally wronged others. Like other men, I loved and hated. I felt joy and sorrow. In short, I lived and drew breath on this earth, doing some good and little wrong.

But I was not happy.

Why did happiness elude me? I was fortunate. I had the love of my family and friends. I had the respect of my peers and my elders; I enjoyed wealth, more than enough to see to the needs of my days and nights.

But I was not happy.

There was something I lacked. I did not know what it was; all I knew was that I was not happy. My mind told me it was because I had not fulfilled certain desires. It told me that I needed power, beautiful women and unending revelry to feel content. It told me that it was these unfulfilled dreams that kept me from my destiny; that kept me from happiness.

Although the desire for these things often burned in my blood and swayed the course of my life, I was lucky enough to realize that these were mostly empty things. Each step I took towards these things was sickening to me; I could see that they were vain and shallow things. I was unhappy with them, but also unhappy without them.

Now I know that my affliction was poverty of the spirit.

If everything that was offered to me wasn't enough to grant me happiness, obviously I needed something more. I needed something permanent, something that brought unending joy, something that brought understanding. Something *real*.

I am an ordinary man, whose one wonder was God.

But if God is everywhere, if God is everything, if God exists throughout time, then why wasn't God in my life? Why couldn't I talk with God? Why couldn't I touch God? Why did I feel so alone and abandoned?

I thought I couldn't speak with God because He was a powerful, neglecting Father, who punished misdeeds but never rewarded just actions. He hated the criminal, but had no pity for victims. He cast us all into perdition. Into exile, to live a fruitless existence of disfigured hopes and crippled dreams. We were told to be thankful that after this imperfect interim period, we would be rewarded for our good deeds, our sacrifice, our belief, with "eternal life." But He couldn't deliver that to us now. And He never spoke to ordinary people, only special ones, his seers; He cut the others like a scythe moving through the fields of grain.

I hated Him.

What kind of God wouldn't speak to an ordinary person? Was I so ugly in his eyes that I didn't deserve a single kind word, one lone act of mercy to show that he loved me? It seemed to me that I had only His irony. Many friends but no real friendship. Many lovers but no true love. I never denied his existence; I knew He existed, and that is why I hated Him. The injustices of the world made me sick, and the indifference of God was the most revolting aspect of all. Imagine that you have the power to feed a starving child, but instead choose to watch her die. Could you be called merciful or just? Would you have the audacity to let others praise you as loving? Where was God in this perpetual tragedy? Where *was* He?

If I could find Him, I would hurt Him for every child that died in pain in front of His eyes. I would usurp the Throne of Heaven and bring joy and wisdom back to our heartbroken and foolish race. I would take His words and His religions in my hand, and I would cast them into the farthest suns, until all that made men hate one another was burnt away.

But the anger that I felt was most acute on my own behalf. Because I wanted God to find me in the darkness, to speak to me. I desired beyond desire to have Him next to me. But He never came.

I screamed so loudly that my body shook; I put my whole heart into the sound, so that if God was alive He would hear me. If God was asleep, He would awaken. And this is what I said: "Where is God in this disgrace? Where is God in this wrong? Where is He for us? Where is He for me?" My breath was ragged. I saw my face in the mirror; it was distorted with rage and pain.

But through all the years of bitterness and emptiness, there was a spark in me that kept the breath in my body. Something inside that allowed me to continue to live, an essence that kept trying to resolve this discord that shattered my heart and crushed the pieces to dust. It was my soul. Beautiful as the stars, strong as a lion, my soul possessed all the wisdom I could never voice. It had all I longed to give birth to, but could not. Like other ordinary men, I knew that I was not the man I wanted to be. I knew that I could be a better man, but I lacked the courage to give words to my wordless dreams and form to my shapeless thoughts.

The clarion call of my soul sounded: "It is a hollow faith that requires constant reassurance. Do you believe God abandons His children in their time of need and sorrow? Do you not know that He is responsible for your daily blessings?"

But I would have none of it, for my anger was at its climax. I said to my soul, "You counsel me to have faith? Why? Is it not said that if something joyous happens it is the will of God, but when malady strikes they say God works in mysterious ways? How is it that He is given credit for our triumphs, and not blamed for our failures? That He is the cause of our joys but not the remover of our sorrows?

Do you not believe that I would rather have faith in a God who loved His children? But the truth does not leave room for ignorance, and your belief is just an illusion. Can you not see that we are abandoned and alone, and that we will die together, you in your blind faith and I in my knowledge?"

And I sobbed alone with my soul until the evening gave way unto the night.

And when my tears were finally spent, I did a simple thing. I looked outside. Through the void of my silent grief came a tremendous joy. I looked at the stars and the trees and I thought, "How beautiful. How beautiful." I heard the sounds of the night and it was a symphony. For the first time in my life there was no thought, no pleasure or pain, there was just peace, and it was heart-wrenchingly perfect.

Then a flood of feeling and emotion engulfed me in an overwhelming intensity that felt like a sun exploding. My consciousness snapped like a branch in strong wind, and my frame began to tremble from this raw, unadulterated power. A pure, full sweet voice spoke: "I am your God, your Light and your Way. And I am joyful that you have come back to me, Son."

Madnesss

And I grew afraid, thinking that I had suddenly embraced madness, and I asked the voice, "How do I know I have not lost my sanity?"

My soul was angry with me. After all the pain I had suffered over those long years, was I foolish enough to question the source of my salvation? "Fool!" it exclaimed. "If this is madness, you should pray to remain insane." I hung my head, ashamed of my fear, but I knew that at that moment there was no other question in my heart.

But the voice of God was gentle.

"Son, who are those set aside as sane or mad? Thoughts beyond the scope of the masses are often reviled, as in a city of fools the wise are ridiculed. In a village of cripples, the one who runs is deemed rash; in a flock of wingless birds, those who soar are cast out. Living without communion with Me is the ultimate madness."

Communion

These words rang true for me, and reverberated through the walls of my heart. But my anger was not resolved. I said to God "Why have you spoken to me now? Bitter were the nights of pain and loneliness when I could have used your counsel and love. Where have You been?

My Soul was disappointed at my impertinence, and exclaimed, "That God chooses to speak to you is enough! What capacity do you have to understand the will of God?"

But the voice of God was kind.

"I have spoken to you for eternity, since before the stars were scattered in the heavens. I come in the peace of stillness, to the tranquil mind. You have not heard my voice because you have grown deaf from sound and thought. You do not clearly hear the calling of a bird, or the sound of silence. If you were placed inside a mountain where even the wind could not disturb you, the roar of your endless thoughts would drown out its peace. You believe that I am finally speaking to you; it is you who are finally listening. Reflect upon this and you will know it to be true. When did you last listen to the voice of the rain?

"I speak to all my children, and have been speaking for eternity. There are those among you who claim that to say you hear the voice of God is blasphemy, but I say that those who do not try to hear my voice are the true blasphemers; they betray Me. They betray life and its most precious gift, which is itself. My Truth is spoken not through those whom I speak to, but those who choose to hear it and repeat it. If only one person in a million is told God's truth, this would make me a callous mother indeed. I speak to the laughing beggar, and I speak to the grim and dour though they are deaf to my voice.

"When you cease your restless agitation and bid me come to you in your heart and soul, then I arrive. I love you; why would I deny you ?"

Purpose

And I asked God, "What then of my purpose in life?
Why am I on this earth?"

My soul grew silent and brooding, for it was ignorant as
I of the reason for these earthly shackles.

The voice of God was like chimes in the breeze. "All
my children are united in purpose, like petals arranged in a
flower, together and separate at once. And the only reason
for your existence is to know Me and to sow love upon this
earth. Bind yourself to love and you join yourself to Me. It
matters not what you do; a parent does not care which game
a child plays, as long as she laughs and smiles. In sowing
love upon the earth, you fulfill the dream that all of Heaven
dreamt when you were born.

Hardship and Pain

I was not yet satisfied. "How can you ask me to love when there is so much pain on this earth? Why did you fashion the darkness, the hate and the anger and place it over the larger heart of life? We are your children; we cry out to you in many voices that are yet one. Where are you in our time of need?"

My soul scolded me like an angry parent. "You dare say that He has created something unbeautiful? The only ugliness on this earth is that which has been wrought by you and your kind."

The voice of God was bright and full of hope, like the sun piercing through the clouds.

"The anguish in you has been put there by your own hands, and I shall open to you the meaning of it. First, know that I am with all My children at all times. I wait, a guest on your doorstep knocking. If you would but open the house of your heart, whose door is silence, I would step over the threshold and gather you up in My arms. As for the suffering in the hearts of man, there are many kinds. There is the pain of the hungry, and the pain of those who are full. There is pain among the rich and pain among the poor. Pain is the ethos of your existence, not because it is so for all things, but because you choose it to be. Your life is chronicled through cycles of joy and loss, sickness and health, failure and success, and you always feel cheated and tried. If you desire an end to suffering, I tell you now to heed these words as a lost traveller is aided by a sign. You seek to deny Me by denying the life that transpires in this moment. I see your dreams: they tell me you are waiting for the time when you will be happy, the time when you will love and be loved, but right now you do not choose to be happy or to love. When your desire is obtained, your thirst is not quenched, but flows on like a river that has burst from a dam.

"Should you wish to end your suffering, begin by realizing that you spend most of your life dreaming of when you will be happy. How can you hear My voice when your thoughts are shouting about your next goal, your most recent defeat?

You are the barrier to your happiness; you are the cause of your own troubles. Seek to understand and conquer this, and then that which you need shall be given to you by the hand of God. And you will see it to be your hand.

You ask me of anger and hate, but what about joy and love? Darkness and light are defined by each other, for how could you know darkness without light? All pleasure that ends gives pain and the end of pain is pleasure. The wounds of your heart brought you to Me on this night; have they not given to you the gift you have prayed for?"

Doubt and Faith

And I then said, "Tell me of doubt and faith. A thousand and one times a day we are given reasons to doubt the goodness of the human heart, and the ultimate justice of life itself. Why should we have faith in anything other than that which we know for certain?"

And my soul gently cried for me. "Do you think God wants you to have faith for God's sake? Do you believe God is magnified by your adoration and lessened by your disbelief? Does the mountain quiver when the ant leaves it? Does the forest cry out when a bird flees from it? If God weeps, it is for what you have lost."

There was silence in the darkness. Then He spoke. "By all means, question and doubt. If it gives you joy to doubt, then doubt; if it brings you peace to doubt, then doubt, if doubt brings you closer to the truth then doubt. But if doubt is not grounded in reason, and it leads you to sadness, to unhappiness, to emptiness, then what is its use to you? Know that there are many mysteries which you cannot fathom with your mind. Can you tell Me what infinity is, or how long eternity? Can you speak truthfully of creation and the end of time? No, you cannot speak of these things; you can barely think of them. But your heart can long for this knowledge, and your soul can feel and touch it. It is your choice to have faith in the infinite and eternal and seek it out, or to remain bound by the limits of human knowledge.

"I desire you to question. When you question the nature of the world, you open your minds to the answers that your souls softly speak. But as you doubt, realize with humility that the great oaks have seen more days and nights then you have, and the stars have burned before the first of you were born and will burn long after the last of you has departed.

"And know that faith does not exist to explain the world. Faith exists to help you live in it."

Sin

And I asked God, "What of sin? I have lain at night in sweet lust. I have taken drink both to enjoy and to escape this world. I am guilty of many things that I have been told were sins against You. Have You not turned Your face from me because of these transgressions?"

My soul whispered to me in painful longing. "I plead with you to find solace in God and me alone. I ask you not because I wish you to avoid sin, but because you search for happiness in empty places."

A thousand trumpets sounded in my mind; a thousand smiles flashed. I heard God laughing. And he said to me, "First be at ease and know that the sins you commit are against yourself. If your soul is weightless after an action, know that you have not committed sin, regardless of what others say. The one who is in touch with eternity through serenity, joy and the wish to spread delight to all, is elevated above laws and rules, for he is governed by love, which never leads one astray. Why should your life be constrained by the fear of sin, when you are beckoned to walk free in joy?

"When you live without Me, you sometimes lose your way. There are times when anger calls to you, intolerance deafens you, rage blinds you. Make no hasty action during this time, because in the throes of such terrible passion you lose the company of reason and it is then you commit what you call "sin." But if God is in your life, if love is your path, then banish your fear of sin and your affection for laws that are like prisons, and be free.

"Beware those who tell you that you are a sinner in My eyes, those who claim to know what is pleasing to me and what is not. It is far better that you speak to me and to your soul to find that which moves you. To those who proclaim that man is weak and so falls into sin, tell them you will hear none of their words, for God bids you to be mindful of virtue so that you may bind yourself more closely to the qualities of your Maker.

"You say that you have taken drink, but I have seen you with your loved ones at sitting at your table, and as the wine flows so does your love. What wrong is there in this?

"There are those who sit sober, proclaiming that because they do not taint their bodies they are closer to the Lord than their brothers and sisters. Their intoxicant is pride; what virtue is in their actions?

"Make no mistake though; as you reap so shall you sow. I have seen you sick with too much pleasure, your soul rebuking you as your body suffers. If you must be overfull with something, then let it be love."

Religion

I marvelled at the genius of the Lord of Creation, but I still contained a lifetime of questions. I asked, "Why have you divided men into different religions, so that they argue and even murder in your name? Why have you not come and declared one religion, one faith that would unite us all, or destroy the idea of religion entirely?"

My soul rose like a wounded serpent and bit me, saying, "Has it not become plain to you that our Master is not the author of any misery on this earth, but that misguided zealots sow destruction in this world? You blame the teachings of religion; I blame the inattentive students who see only the flesh of the fruit and not the seeds." I grew pensive at my soul's scolding.

The voice of God was hurt, and I felt guilty for offending the only one in my life who would walk with me forever. And the Almighty said, "Your words pain bitterly, not because you ask, but because it is a valid question. Why do those who magnify my name smear it with blood? How shall I speak to those who proclaim God's majesty so loud that they drown out My peace? Nothing causes My heart to ache more than unloving acts committed in the misguided belief that they are pleasing to Me. Remember always love. Do nothing against love and you will always follow God's truest teachings.

"You ask me why there are so many religions, and I tell you that in the garden of My heart grow innumerable flowers, all known to me, all dear to me. Why should My garden be adorned with only roses, or lotuses or jasmine? Should not they all float their perfumed scents to Heaven?

"Blessed be the people who say 'I am a Christian, or a Hindu, Muslim or Jew' and strive to follow the tenets of their faith. But the wise sons and daughters of Life declare 'I am a Christian, a Muslim, a Hindu and a Jew. I am a child of God, and unto all altars do I kneel, for the Lord is not contained within one house, as the rain does not fall on a single patch of land.'"

Time

And I said, "Song and symphony, what of time? Does it not take the innocent and carefree children and turn them into defeated old women and men, whose dreams have been abandoned and loves forsaken? Does it not murder the passion of the young, and give nothing in return? My Lord, I fear the loss of my love, my dreams and my vitality. I fear the bitterness and cynicism that time brings. I only wish to be gathered to Your hand before my heart hardens, and I no longer know how to speak or play with children."

My soul answered my questions sharply. "Time does not murder passion, love or truth; men butcher their own lives when they regard the values of others. Look into your world and you will see those who traded their dreams for comfort and sold their loves for respect. Live the life you wish to, unfettered by the bonds that your countrymen, you brethren and, yea, even your family would lay upon you. For parents may not claim their children's lives so that they might live their deferred dreams, and it is not to your countrymen that you owe principal fealty. First you must be true to me and to God, for you will only rest among the stars when you have discharged that note that life has bid you sing."

And I was silent after my soul's words, for their truth both stung and soothed me.

And then God spoke. "If you always follow your soul, you will never lose your dreams or your passion. For it is not youth that bestows these things but Life. And Life does not take passion from the old, but gives it still in full. And wisdom arrives to sit beside passion, making life that much more enchanting. Those who abandoned their dreams and cast aside their loves did so from fear. Their heart was in the Heavens, but their trepidation bound them to the earth.

"My child, time is an illusion. You believe that there is a yesterday and a tomorrow because you have memories of tomorrows that became yesterdays. You have taken something which you cannot feel or see, and broken it down and down until you can understand it. You take the hours and make them minutes, and make the minutes seconds. You make the days weeks, and the weeks months, and the months years. But can you tell me what a moment feels like? How long is it? How long is a minute to a man who is drowning? How long is an hour with the beloved?

"Why would you capture time? Why cut your days and nights into pieces that are scattered to the wind, fragments of memory and desire? There is only one moment in time and that is now. For yesterday is a memory and tomorrow is a dream; we think of yesterday at this moment and dream of tomorrow in this moment."

Mercy

I marvelled at the vision of this most gifted Artist, and asked, "Sun of my sky, tell me of mercy. What is it and why should I be merciful? For my brethren on this earth are often a hateful, spiteful lot who harm me and others. Why should I be merciful when none show mercy to me?"

My soul said to me in a voice filled with pity, "None shows mercy to you? That you wake and breathe, that you have been given days and nights, that there is food on your table, what greater mercy is there then this? How could you even exist on this earth without the ultimate mercy of the Lord of Life?"

The voice of God was summer to my winter. He said, "Dear one, know that men will cheat you. Know that men will rob from you, they will slander you, and they will spurn you. Show them mercy. By showing them mercy you do something pleasing to My eye, and for your own soul. Son, they know not what they do, and even were they to know what pain they inflicted upon you, let it be, for no real harm can come to you. Your possessions will be taken by death, your name will be forgotten, but you will walk with Me through death and eternal life. If others do you wrong, and their wrongdoing reminds you of this, they have in fact done you tremendous good.

"Mercy is not an action, it is an attitude. When you are grateful to awaken to the morning and to go to sleep at night, when you find contentment in the air you breathe, the silence you hear, and the beauty you behold, you will do as little harm as you can in this world, and forgive others their transgressions. When you realize that every day Life bestows upon you a treasure so great that it cannot be traded for anything in the entire world, you cannot be anything but merciful. Mercy does not relieve others of the consequences of their actions, but by sowing love instead of anger, you make a lotus grow in the mud, a rose rise from the stones. Is there any greater miracle than this?"

Fame and Power

To my Master I then admitted shamefully, "I desire fame and power. I wish my name to be magnified in the records of time, like a Caesar. I want to have power in this world, and be praised. Please forgive me."

I huddled in fear, for my soul flared and crackled like a wildfire that threatens to destroy the entire forest. It said to me, "Better that you perish by your own hand then become another butcher in the pages of history, who builds palaces over the bones of his brothers. And though you live in a world that praises tyrants and ridicules poets, know that the laws of Life judge harshly a man who values power and fame over the beauty of each sunrise. Your desires are baser then your essence. Why would you mix gold with dross?"

But the voice of God was patient, like a new mother with a crying infant. "There is never a need to ask forgiveness from me. Every pardon is granted, every mistake is forgiven. I withhold nothing from you. Your desires do not offend me; they offend your soul. Your desires are not wrong, but they are beneath you. As a child playing with a lit candle is terrifying to the eyes of a parent, so is your soul disturbed by your desire for these things, yet they are not wrong, not unnatural. Life is more than simple existence.

"Yet realize that this is not what you truly desire. You desire fulfillment and her sisters, happiness and contentment, and you do not know where to find them, and so you search the treasury of the transient instead of that greater one that I have opened up for you: the treasury of Life. Turn to me and ask for what you need to feel supremely joyous, and I will surely give it to you. It is the highest prize, and is given to kings and beggars unconditionally alike: Myself. How long you wish to labour in the temporary field of pleasure and pain before coming to the Valley of Eternal Joy is entirely up to you.

"You say to me 'I desire to have my name in the books of history,' and I tell you that eternity carries all away. No life leaves any mark on this earth, save that which was made with love. Though your books contain the actions and words of other men, know that their essence has long departed, and that in the eyes of God no one life was ever worth more then another, as a shepherd does not favour one sheep above the rest of the flock. All that I wish is for you to be coherent of life's majesty and splendour, to be awake, with your head turned toward the sky instead of at your feet, and with your eyes settling on the horizon and knowing that all is beautiful and perfect. For Life is to be lived, not recorded, and I am most pleased when you simply enjoy it."

Evil

My soul and I were being awakened unto a morning that had not yet dawned, but I felt so confident of God's continued generosity that I asked, "Father, what of evil? What is that which divides nations and families, leaving nothing but ruin? What of that which leaves such grisly scars on the face of history that it sickens us to be members of humankind?"

The Lord stared at the naked recesses of my being before He spoke. It felt like my soul was being unraveled and the layers of my pain shed like old skin. The voice of God was soft, like a child's breath in front of a flickering candle. "Have I not said that darkness and light come together? So do your notions of good and evil. For evil to you is good to your enemies. And those whom you deem your enemies are not the soulless, hateful, ignorant beings you paint them as, but rather your friends cloaked in disguise. A diamond and a coal are not as different as they appear to be. There are very few who are so lost in darkness that they abandon what makes them human and become truly mad. Most of those whom you believe are evil are simply wandering in confusion, as you too often wander. The rebel and the hero are often the same person seen through different eyes; the truth is that they are both and neither.

"The greatest evils in your world are committed by those who believe they do the greatest good. Nothing is more dangerous than someone who is convinced of her own unerring righteousness. Always question your actions, and let your soul be your magistrate. Submit to its acquittals and learn from its sentences. Summon reason and love to guide you, and let silence, both that of your surroundings and that of your thoughts, be your constant teacher.

Science and Knowledge

And then I asked, "Infinite Love, tell me now of science and knowledge. For there are those who say it is an affront to your words, while others says it is the light to the darkness of our own ignorance. Some claim it proves You are the refuge of fools and zealots, and had no part in the making of our universe."

And my soul reprimanded me, saying, "And what is it to you what these others say? For those who heed foolish counsel are worse than those who speak it. Who can deny the magnificence of creation; why does it matter how the Lord fashioned Life? Your capacity to understand the mind of God is that of an impertinent child who questions the behaviour of his father."

But the voice of God entered swiftly and surely, like the north wind through the trees. "May you indeed probe the vastness of creation and see Me in the glory of its simplicity, and in its magnificent complexity, its endless secrets. May you see Me in rock and tree and atom and cell, and proclaim the terrible beauty of creation. There is a purity to knowledge; the feeling of enlightenment at the appreciation of an aspect of this world brings joy to the soul. This is another one of Life's great gifts. Many of your greatest thinkers had tender moments gazing at infinity; their portion of divine understanding gave them a profound appreciation for Life. Why should you decry this as sinful and blasphemous?

"Examine the laws of existence and search for answers, for both the search and the results are beautiful, but know that you have existed longer then the short days and nights that you awaken to and dream in. Your first breath was taken when the stars flared and the heavens wheeled, and that craving in you to know your universe is yourself hungering for another taste of infinity.

"Never fear the questions you ask or the answers you find, for the answer to the most important question of your existence is this: I know and love each of you."

Fate

Then I looked outside at the stars which blazed in the night sky, and asked, "Master of my days and nights, what then of fate? For it is whispered that men are like fallen leaves scattered by Your divine wind. Others contend that there is nothing greater than humankind, which has shaped the world to its will."

And my soul derisively spat out this: "Praise be to the day when God brings you to pain and sorrow, for in your imperfect knowledge you either believe She does not love you and leads you to suffering, or She does not exist and that is why you suffer. To believe there is no greater author in life than humankind is like being a sailor who reckons the end of the horizon the edge of the earth."

The voice of God was soothing, like cool water over a burn. "Know that I hear the words of those who say they are powerless and those that reckon themselves all powerful. I hold both in my hand, and love them equally. That you believe that the ending to the story of your life is already written is true: You die. Then you live again. Plenty and dearth, joy and sorrow; you cycle endlessly through them while you labour on this earth. But if the ending, death, is known to you, what you do not know is the actual shape your life will take. You and your soul are the principal authors of your destiny, and I am the page upon which you write. Should you wish to escape this never-ending story, which has differed only in minor details since life began, then find God in your life. For this is the only notable event in your novel; this is the climax of the entirety of creation, a soul awakening to see and know itself in all its glory. This is where eternity begins for you.

"The end of your life is not your salvation; the living of it is."

Wealth

And I asked, "Lord, tell me now of wealth. We have been told that accumulation of wealth is both desirable and wrong. What do You say of wealth and poverty?"

My soul spoke gently. "You ask of wealth and poverty, but know you not that this discourse is the greatest wealth, and any desire outside communion with God the greatest poverty?"

Yet the voice of God was even more gentle. "It is more than permissible to ask me of wealth and poverty. Because your world judges people according to what they possess, you wonder about the significance of wealth, what it means to Me. In truth, it is not of any consequence to Me. I care not for the wealth of your belongings but for the love of your heart. Virtue is what God places into each man, rich or poor, and there it remains forever.

"But let your mind be at ease; there is nothing wrong with being rich or poor. Therefore, if you seek wealth and search for it gently, taking nothing at the cost of another, then you shall find it with my blessings. If you seek wealth out of greed, know that you will find it, but it will never satisfy your deepest hunger. One can have everything and still feel nothing.

"Yet, if God is your succor and refuge, if God is your dearest confidant, and most trusted benefactor, then why should you be afraid to approach Me and ask for wealth? If I am the One Who will open the gates of Heaven to you, then why would I not open the vaults of the earth as well? Ask me, with a pure heart full of need rather than an unhappy mind full of want, and it shall be given to you; simply believe. Blessed is the one who has known both want and plenty, and awakens to either saying, 'Praise be to this day, that I arise by the grace of God.'"

Justice

Gratefulness overtook me, but curiosity drove me on. I asked, "Please tell me, what is Justice? We are imperfect beings who make imperfect laws; how might we treat each other, and the earth, justly?"

My soul said quietly, "Justice is looking into the hearts of the criminal and the victim, and realizing that they both have injured and been injured. If your heart bleeds for the lion as well as the deer, you will be guided always to justice."

And God said, "Loving child, your soul guides you to the nature of justice. Justice is not vengeance, it is not punishment, it is simple reaction. Justice is an ever-present principle, which holds sway over the mechanisms of creation. You judge the wolf that kills your lamb a murdering beast, but in its heart it does no wrong. It feels no remorse for the lamb, because it does nothing against its own truth, its own soul. If you tremble when you are to about to taste meat, and your soul cries out in protest, then put it away and go to your garden to find sustenance that does stain your soul with guilt. And if your brother sees the same meat, and in his heart is a prayer of thanksgiving that he may eat and live, then let him eat, and judge him not. Remember always that the soul of each person has its own truth, and even if that truth is not yours, embrace it and do not slight it, for it too is a part of Me.

"True justice requires understanding that every crime contains two essential elements: the wrongs the criminal has suffered at the hands of society or other individuals, and the wrongs that the victim suffers. You are not divorced from the misdoings of your brothers and sisters; if they steal out of need, then you have all failed. If they have transgressed your laws, it is often because they too have been transgressed against. Justice prevails not when every criminal is jailed, but when each person takes it to be his duty to assuage the hunger of his sisters and brothers.

Yet, to everyone has God given choice. Though you have received pain from the hands of Life, you can choose to not visit that pain onto another, but to hold it and caress it, and transform it into the inner fire that will warm you. Every man is responsible for his choices in life, and though you must often shoulder great burdens, and cry to the Heavens, "Why me, Lord?" you should still seek to do good. For evil given in return for evil received is not justice, it is blindness. In your soul there flows a tremendous power to change all pain into joy, as an alchemist turns lead into gold. When life passes you pain accept it, for with effort it will become your teacher, bringing you to joy and to Me.

For as Life is supremely just, giving to all their days and nights, so must you endeavor to give as you receive from Me."

Loneliness

I paused for a moment and unearthed my deepest pain, and with bleeding fingers said, "My God, I am alone. Although I have friends and family in abundance, their speech brushes my surface but does not stir my core. Upon this earth, I have only my soul to keep me company. It is a beautiful and poetic thing, even if it is sometimes harsh as it spurs me on towards You. But in the day, as I walk alone, I think, "How beautiful it would be, if I able to walk in this place with my beloved. One who loved me and understood my pain. One who would willingly carry my cross for a day. One whom I could touch and who would touch me, one whom I could speak with and listen to. I am alone, Mother; could you not in your mercy send someone to fill the gap in my heart?"

The anger of my soul was paramount. "Alone? I am your *soul*, your eternal companion throughout life and death. That you cannot be satisfied that I am with you, and that the Infinite is with you in spirit and flesh, dooms you to a loneliness that cannot be changed by the mere presence of another."

But at the sound of God's voice, every cell in my body seemed to be singing and this collective harmony built to a glorious crescendo that made my heart laugh and my spirit dance before it calmed to silence. "I *know* your pain. It is the pain of a blade of grass which considers itself separate from other blades. But could you not say to the grass, 'You are a blade among blades; alone you are grass and together you are grass'? Would you not say to a drop of water in the sea, 'You are an ocean in a drop and a drop in an ocean'? Because the desert is not but grains of sand, and each grain is a desert.

"You are alone simply because you believe yourself to be alone. You must awaken unto the world and see that you are not only connected to it, you compose it. Your heart and the heart of Creation beat as One, because they have been both wrought by the hand of Life. You are not separate from Me or your soul, for I fashioned you out of the only thing in existence, which is Myself.

"You have already begun to awaken to this truth; in communion with your soul and Me, you will arise one day and feel Life pulsing in the mountains and valleys, and you will know it that it is the same Life that courses through your own heart. And then you will never feel alone again."

Death

In the distance I heard the ominous hooting of an owl. The sound compelled me to ask, "Kind illuminator, tell me now of death. For all must taste death: some with sweet joy, others with bitter sorrow; some with indifference. Some see it approaching, while others are snatched suddenly from us. What of death, which takes our beloved ones and ends our sojourn on this earth?"

My soul, bright with hope, said, "Oh yes, Father and Creator, Mother and Protector, what of death? For I long to behold Your face and grasp Your hand in eternity once again. I wish to journey beyond the stars and into the heart of Your most brilliant suns. And though my charge feels my joy, he is sometimes in fear of the end, which will see his loved ones fall in the flesh but soar in spirit. I crave to see the face that will deliver me to eternity. In sleep I am at peace, but I long to be free always. Know that I long for you as the desert longs for the sweet rain."

And God, in a voice pure as a child's, said "You are *always* with Me. These long years without communion have given you a terrible thirst, but now I am here and will quench it. As you said, there are three ways in which people look towards death; with joy, indifference or fear. Those who view it with indifference have grown tired, and long for change. And change is the one thing that is assured in this world.

"What of those who look at death with fear? What do you say to the one who fears his end? You say that all true things never perish. Tell him that Life, Truth, Justice and Love never fade from this world as they do from the hearts of humankind. Tell him that his soul, which is fashioned from the stars, lives forever in the Garden of Eternity, where it finds nourishment in itself and Me. Assure him that Life passes through seasons, and that after winter comes the spring again. If he cannot understand you, tell him to be at ease and have faith, for the mystery of how life comes to this world and how it leaves this world is a secret yet.

"Those who look to death with love are intimately known to me, for their prayers burn with a fire that sets your world alight. They seek Me as their beloved, and long for the moment when I will touch them. At that instant they will know unbound joy, unrestrained love and eternal peace.

"My Hands accept all, but it is my desire that all seek me out now, so that they will have the peace of knowing I walk with them over the vast mountains of Life and through the slender valley of death.

"You ask me of the nature of death, which robs you of the ones you love and places in your heart bitter pain and the worm of fear. But whom do you weep for? Do you weep for the one who has been gathered into My arms? Do you weep for the soul that knows no more earthly conflict, that watches you from near and far, transcending time and space? Or do you weep for yourself? Why do you not contemplate that which made those who go before you so dear, and then move on, swearing to honour always that which you loved most in them? For bodies perish but souls live on. People pass, but the love they give and take is everlasting. Never look to the dead with pity, for there are none to whom death is an affliction; like Life, it is a blessing. Only the fear of death can mask its glory, as the blur of the stars hide their true light.

Truth

"Supreme Protector," I called, "what is truth? What is the truth of existence, the truth of life? What is the truth of reality, action, and love?

And my soul whispered, "I am truth. You are truth. God is truth."

But I was confused by my soul's cryptic words, and beseeched the Lord to answer. And God gently brushed the urge in my heart, and at once I knew peace. He said, "I understand your urge to know truth. Know that your soul does not mock you with its words, but gives you the knowledge which you seek. It speaks to your ears things which you deem strange, but these things are as close to the truth as words may come. You wish to hear this is truth or that is truth, but truth is more simple than that. It is as subtle as the razor's edge, as gross as the mountains. Truth is the essential element of all things; it is that which comprises all creation. Truth is that with no opposite.

"Truth is silence when you listen to it, love when you feel it, life when you live it, time when you understand it.

39

If the idea of truth confounds you, then do not think of it, for she is elusive to most, although she is always in front of them. Those who find her leave the world of humankind though they still live and breathe. She is the poet's dearest lover and bitterest foe, for she puts into them a single word they will spend an eternity trying to utter, until they awaken and realize they are that word. And if this sounds strange to you, let it be, for truth will be spoken only when she is ready to be spoken, as the morning comes only after the long hours of the night."

Weakness

My soul said, "Water of Life, your love has brought me back to strength. But I ask you now to counsel on weakness. For I know my charge will fall again and again, seduced by the thoughts he himself has given birth to. How may I lead him out of the cave of his making?"

And God said kindly, "Know that all men fall into weakness and doubt. That they do so endlessly in life and again in death is no new occurrence. Be patient and steadfast; steer him always into the path shared by you and his heart. For although he is his own enemy, he is also his own benefactor. As is he weak, so is he strong. He may reject your counsel time and again, but give it still, for when he hears you and decides to dedicate himself to following, then he will cease to be a man and become what he was born to be. He walks with you crying or runs from you laughing, but one day he will embrace you and then conflict will cease, and pain will end. Two will come as one unto Me and unite that which thought has rent asunder."

God

For the first time, my soul and I spoken in unison. "Beloved and Majestic One. Most Merciful and Praiseworthy One. Father and Mother, Lover and Friend, I ask you for the ultimate knowledge. I ask you now what we have asked for centuries, what we crave to know. Lord of Lords, King of Creation, Time and Life, what are You? Where do You reside?"

And the presence of God grew to a magnitude that made me tremble underneath the night sky. Pictures of vast endless space filled my mind; my breath quickened and my heart beat faster in anticipation of the end. My blood ran to all corners of my body; my soul drank in ecstasy. The sun was abstract and small, then alive and large beyond even the capacity of my mind's eye to see it. Quickly, too quickly, I went wheeling towards it. Then the sun was eclipsed by the vastness of space, which kept drinking in more and more planets, and even entire galaxies. I could not even fathom an end to this spectacle?, which was terrifying in its splendour and instantly humbling. I had no sense of myself. I didn't exist. I was so small and so helpless. Any last vestige of arrogance I had was shredded by these visions. I remember hearing my voice cry out, a wordless yell at magnificence that would surely destroy me.

And then it stopped. There were no thoughts, there were no feelings, there was just the sound of my own breathing. Shallow and rapid at first, but then slower and deeper. Slowly I came back to myself, and when I regained my composure, the voice of God spoke calmly and deliberately. It was the voice of a parent lovingly reassuring a child.

"Before there was time, I was. Before there was space, I was. Before there was light, before there was darkness, before there was void, I was. I am the eternal, the never-ending. I am here, I am there, and I am the space in between. I am the source of existence, for how could existence be without something to give it birth?

"I am all that is. I am that which makes the darkness and light, the day and the night. I am your purest thoughts and noblest virtues. I am justice, truth, passion, love, death, and life. I am the laws of creation, and the Maker of the laws. I am your Maker and I am what composes you. I am all that is and was, and all that will come to pass. I am the message and the speaker, I am the fire and the light; I am the single note of the single song that spun the stars, the sky and the suns.

"I am beyond words and thoughts, but not beyond the comprehension of your soul.

"And if this remains a riddle to you till the end of your life, then be content with it, for you ask an answer to a question so boundless it cannot be fully voiced. And though it mystifies you and challenges you, and sometimes angers you, know that one day the answer of Life will arrive. On that day your journey will be over, because it will be the day you realize it never began. Because you have never strayed from the hand or love of God."

Morning

I wept softly into the dying night, while the sun began to usher in a new day. And I said, "Please, do not leave me now. But rather take me, a grape in Your vineyard, and pluck me from the vine of life. I lived in madness before You spoke to me, and now I fear beyond fear that I may lose You and the wisdom You have given me tonight. Do not cast me alone back into the world, but put my hand into the hand of eternity, for I desire never to violate Your love for me and my love for my soul. I will make any sacrifice, but please let not us be separated, even by sleep."

And God said, with such intense love that I will never know the equal of it as long as I live, "I have called you many names tonight, but none more sacred then that which I called you first: My Son. I have never left your side or the side of any of my children. At all places, at all times you will hear my voice. There is nothing you can do that will turn My heart from yours. This communion is available to you always, as it is to your brothers and sisters. You will feel it as surely as you feel the sun on your face. And whenever truth fades from your heart, know that I will send it again and again, until you come back to Me. Embrace the beauty of sleep and dreams now, for they will give you the strength to love this coming day.

"Sleep peacefully child; I am with you."

I closed my eyes, with a prayer of thanksgiving on my lips for everything that had brought me to this moment. The sun was being born in the east, the first tips of its brilliance brightening the darkness. The birds had not yet awakened, but a warm breeze blew, carrying to me the last words of the night before I passed into sleep.

"Sleep peacefully child; I am with you."

About the Author

Nikhil Joshi, a young writer, an orator, a Canadian chess champion, and a philosopher asks thought provoking questions about life, relationships and about spirituality in his book, *The Companion*.

As a Millennium Laureate, Nikhil has been nationally recognized by the Government of Canada for his leadership skills and for his work in improving the lives of youths experiencing challenges due to their social, economic and cultural backgrounds in St. John's, Newfoundland and Labrador. His recent volunteer work took him to Ghana, Africa where he was working to help treat and prevent HIV, as well as teach English as a second language.

He has a background in broadcasting and worked as a freelance journalist for five years with the Canadian Broadcasting Corporation (CBC). His media-based company, *Youth of the Nation* was featured nationally on the television show *Street Cents*. Currently, he splits his time between attending University at the University of Calgary, volunteering with various charities, such as the Centre for Integral Economics, and conducting healthcare research with the Western Canada Waiting List Project. Working with his co- researchers, his article entitled "Health Care Guarantees: Necessity or Nemesis?" was recently published in June 2006 edition of the scholarly journal *Healthcare Management*.

Nikhil is passionate about furthering his ability to touch the lives of people positively. He currently lives in Calgary, Alberta, Canada.

Printed in the United States
64948LVS00001B/28-126